Text
Forms
and
Features

A Resource for Intentional Teaching

Margaret E. Mooney

Richard C. Owen Publishers, Inc.
Katonah, New York

RICHARD C. OWEN PUBLISHERS, INC.
PO Box 585
Katonah, New York 10536

Library of Congress Cataloging-in-Publication Data

Mooney, Margaret E.
    Text forms and features: a resource for intentional teaching/Margaret E. Mooney.
        p. cm.
    Includes bibliographical references and index.
    ISBN 1-57274-456-1 (pbk.)
    1. Reading. 2. Literary form—Study and teaching. I. Title.
LB1050.2 .M66 2001
428.4—dc21

                                                          2001021335
                                                                CIP

Printed in the United States of America

9   8   7   6   5   4   3

Acknowledgment

An earlier edition of this manuscript was developed for the Office of the Superintendent of Public Instruction in Washington State. The author gratefully acknowledges teachers' comments to and confirmation of that work.

Table of Contents

Foreword

I had just stuffed a bleached cow skull into a box along with a handful of paintbrushes, some frayed pieces of burlap, and a packet of bulletin board letters. Such is the behavior of a teacher dismantling his classroom for the summer. I was eyeing a thirty-gallon fish tank filled with giant tadpoles, each swimming about in a different metamorphic state on its way to full bullfrog maturity. How on earth was I going to persuade my wife to let me keep them in our garage all summer? What would I do with the tank of crickets on which the mature frogs fed? And what about poor Mildred, the salad-plate–sized Argentine frog that spent her days in a smaller tank perched atop a heating pad? Worse yet, what about the cage of perpetually perpetuating field mice on which Mildred fed?

A ringing phone provided reprieve from these nagging questions. On the other end of the line was a person from the Office of Superintendent of Public Instruction for Washington State. She wondered if I would be interested in helping with a series of institutes for elementary teachers during the coming summer. Margaret Mooney would be working with the teachers to develop a cadre of solidly trained mentors who in turn would help train teachers in their own school districts over the next two or three years. Would I be interested in facilitating small group discussion with these teachers as they were being trained by Margaret? I gasped. A tadpole splashed. Mildred let out a bark. I uttered an excited and nervous "yes," and the world turned upside down.

Several weeks later on the campus of Western Washington University, one hundred teachers and reading specialists came together for their first institute. To observe Margaret Mooney with a room full of teachers is to see the very art of teaching itself. She can bring a group to the edge of their chairs and to the cusp of their own understanding in a flash. Once there, Margaret advises, challenges, probes, and propels her audiences to ever deeper understandings of their own profession and practice. With the delicacy and precision of a scalpel and the force of a jackhammer, Margaret asks questions. "How does the structure of your classroom and your use of time reflect your personal philosophy of reading instruction?" "Whose room is it anyway, yours or theirs?" "During guided reading, how does the text form support meaning making?" "Are your struggling readers needy, or worthy?" "Who is responsible for children learning to read? The products and books you buy, or you, the teacher who uses them?"

Traditionally, elementary students have been raised on a fare of fantasy fiction. Margaret challenged the teachers with whom she worked to question that practice. If students were going to be expected to master more complex text forms by fourth grade, then why shouldn't they be exposed to them in kindergarten? If we were going to expose students to the same text forms they would be encountering later in life, which forms and what about each of them should we teach?

To these questions teachers offered a variety of answers with varying degrees of self-assurance and self-doubt. After all, these were teachers who had been acknowledged by their peers and administrators as outstanding. Each came with a solid reputation and a history of successful teaching. Yet each was challenged by Margaret's questions. Never had they been asked to define their beliefs about literacy instruction so precisely, or to articulate exactly how those beliefs were made manifest in their daily interactions with students.

Intermingled with these questioning sessions, Margaret taught techniques for shared and guided reading. The group marveled at her ability to instruct. In doing so, she used this same questioning strategy, but changed the focus to the reading act. "If I tell you we are about to read a biography, what do you already know about the text?" "How does this information help you to make meaning of the text?" "How does the author manifest his or her biases as the text progresses?" "To what extent are biography and autobiography alike?" "In what context is one more appropriate than the other as a reading selection?" As the group formulated responses to these questions, Margaret pushed them further still. Each answer was greeted with a smile, a nod, and a quizzical prod: "And what else?" That summer Margaret stretched each of us to the very limits of our own understanding.

I returned to my classroom the following fall feeling like a first-year teacher. How could I incorporate all of Margaret's strategies and questioning techniques into my reading instruction? Why was I putting the bleached cow skull up? Which expository texts would I house next to the tadpole tank and which by Mildred? As so often happens, some of these questions answered themselves. For one, poor Mildred met her demise when an overly large mouse got stuck in her throat. The first graders and I buried her in a pizza box with all the pomp and circumstance that her noble girth deserved. Seven-year-old Cory summed her life up best during his inspiring eulogy: "Mildred was a good frog, but she was a bad pig. That's why she's dead."

I've always been a "good" teacher, but that year I become a purposeful one. As a result, my students' reading skills and strategies and their ability to articulate their own reading behaviors were deeper and richer than anything I'd seen in nearly twenty years of classroom experience. My teaching was more focused, intentional, and self-reflective than ever. As I met with the reading cadre and Margaret throughout the school year, I heard stories similar to my own from every participant. Margaret's teaching had made a profound difference for everyone.

Throughout the following couple of years, as we worked with Margaret and the teacher leaders from Washington State, a common frustration was expressed over and over. In their preservice training, teachers had not focused on the variety of genres and text features that we were expecting our students to master. As such, they were spending an inordinate amount of time seeking appropriate texts and making links between them. Most felt their instruction lacked the depth it could have because of a gap in their own experience as readers and as teachers of reading. As always, Margaret's response was decisive, deep, and completely practical. She developed a manual of text forms and features to serve as a guide for Washington State teachers facing this dilemma. This book is an elaboration and continuation of that earlier work.

In the past few years, teachers and publishers have risen to the challenge of providing elementary students with a rich array of fiction and nonfiction texts. Similar to Margaret's incredible teaching style, this reference book gives classroom teachers the information they need to make the best of those texts. It then challenges them to push further and to extend their skills even deeper. As with all her work, Margaret's questions ring loud and clear throughout this volume. "Here is the information you need about text forms and features and how they work together. Now, what are you going to do with it? And what else?"

The very best teachers share more than information and classroom experience with their students. They inspire and provoke thought and introspection. They deliver just the right amount of support and challenge for each stage of cognitive metamorphosis. They model both the excitement and the satisfaction of learning. In short, they change lives. Margaret Mooney is just such a teacher!

Jerry Miller

Preface

"What book are you currently reading?" the interviewer asked.

"*The History of Lacemaking*," I replied without hesitation.

The air fell silent, eyebrows were raised, and then a series of meaningful glances were exchanged between the four interviewers.

"No, what novel are you reading?," one of the four asked, as if trying to offer me a chance to redeem myself.

Undaunted, I blurted out, "My main reading is books on lacemaking." More meaningful glances signaled a hasty end to the interview.

As I left the room, I pondered their reaction to my choice of reading matter. Would I have had a better chance of being invited to take up the position if I had suggested a book on reading, or editing, or, as prompted, a novel?

Ultimately I was offered and accepted the job—a six-month position that turned into nine years of hard work and enlightenment as I became involved in the development of the revision of the original *Ready to Read* series.[1] But the reaction to my reading habits continued to nag at me. Was something wrong with preferring

---

[1] The *Ready to Read* series is the New Zealand national reading program for the teaching of reading in the early years.

nonfiction? It has always been my preference. After all, I had seen my father devour manuals and technical books with as much enthusiasm as my mother showed toward fiction.

One of the first tasks in my new position was to review the range of material used for the teaching of reading in our schools, especially that used in the first three years. As I pursued that task, my thoughts often went back to the interviewers' questioning response as I realized that the greater proportion of material (at that time, at least 80 percent) used in the name of "teaching reading" was fiction and the majority of that was fantasy fiction. What about the children who did not enjoy fiction? And what about those whose imagination was shaped by a culture or set of values different from that considered the norm? What if the child was more interested in reading about the what and why and how of the world than about make-believe characters in imagined situations?

As I pondered that issue, another thought struck me. The fourth year of school brings with it the expectation that children are competent readers and writers of a wide range of nonfiction forms. They are not only expected to be competent readers in order to gain information but are also assessed on their ability to process and represent that information in reports, essays, charts, tables, paragraphs, and summaries. And what is more, they need to be able to do so across a range of curriculum subjects.

"You only get out of the bank the equivalent of what you have put in," became my theme song and has continued to influence the way I approach both the selection and presentation of material as well as the focus of my teaching. If we want a well-rounded story from our beginning writers we need to show them what a well-rounded story is, how it is structured, and how they can do likewise. How many times in those early school years do we expect our students to be able to retell a story, write a report, or recount an experience without being shown how? We need to follow the teaching sequence for writing just as we do for reading, i.e., planning, observing, and adjusting our demonstrations, guides, and prompts to enable the children to observe, absorb, practice, and produce at their appropriate level of competence. This includes writing reports, retellings, summaries, poems, lists, letters, diaries, journals—whatever we expect our children to write—for them, explicitly explaining our thoughts as we compose and draft the text. Then we need to create opportunities for them to participate in many shared writing lessons before "flying solo under supervision" in guided writings. Only then do we have the right to anticipate seeing pieces of work nearing our expectations.

The plethora of eight-page books now available for beginning readers offers far more than practice in repetition and prediction. Many of them enable children to understand (even if in a rudimentary degree) the essential elements of a range of different text forms and provide examples of techniques authors use to capture the reader's interest. Without "doing a book to death" or taking away the joy of discovering the humor, twist, subplot, or climax for oneself, showing children how reading is "writing in the head" and writing is "reading through the pen," we can give real credence to our claim that reading and writing are interdependent processes.

"Walking the talk" has become a catch-cry, but I am not sure that we have really caught the thought behind platitudes about links between reading and writing or aims of developing "life-long readers." Some questions requiring honest answers by authors, publishers, administrators, test designers, and teachers could include:

- What kinds of reading and writing will our students do once they leave the education system?

  (A reality check would be to compare responses with our own reading and writing habits. For example, what have you read and written during the past 24 hours? What proportion was for sheer pleasure, and how much was to survive in your job, your household, and your world?)

- How often are curriculum disciplines other than reading and writing assessed through reading and writing?

- How much instructional reading and writing time is devoted to helping students understand the function and nature of text types and the reader or writer's role in each?

- What is the ratio of fiction/nonfiction material used when assessing progress in reading and writing?

- What is the ratio of fiction/nonfiction material available within the school for instructional purposes or for children to choose to read?

- How much money was spent on resources for reading compared with that spent for writing?

- How much material was purchased in book form and how much provided examples of "real-world reading," costing nothing other than time for collecting?

It is hoped that this resource will provide prompts of the breadth and depth of the material students will probably be expected to understand and comprehend or create. The first chapter outlines some ways in which the book could be used. This is followed by an alphabetical listing of text forms or types, each detailed under the subheadings of "why," "what," and "features." As with all sections of this resource, the list of text forms or text types is not intended to be definitive but is representative of the main ways in which authors present their ideas and information. Diagrams providing examples of ways in which text types can be grouped are followed by reminders of some of the techniques the author uses to engage readers. The final section is an alphabetical listing of some text and book conventions and organizational techniques. These have been selected to give general rather than complete coverage and, as with the section on text forms, are listed under the subheadings of "why," "what," and "features."

Chapter 1

So, Why This Text?

This book is designed to be a resource for "dipping and delving" rather than a book to be read in sequence or a "how-to" manual or curriculum guide. The information is not definitive, nor is it specific or exclusive to any grade level, set of materials, or teaching approach. The items within any entry are not listed in any hierarchy and a strong plea is made that the entries should not be used as a checklist or that students be required to be familiar with all of the features or purposes of any particular text form. Teachers will need to make their own decisions about the most appropriate text and the depth of understanding of its function and nature suitable for the competence of the students and the purpose of the task.

It is strongly recommended that students should first have experience with the various text forms and features through hearing them read, seeing them composed, and through reading and writing them in supported and guided situations before being expected to read or write similar forms on their own. The book *Intentional Teaching: Guided Reading Beyond Grade 3* (Mooney, in press) will provide an in-depth look at this instructional approach.

It is anticipated that this book will have several uses, including:

- Reminding teachers of the nature and purpose of a range of text forms;
- Reassessing the range and use of material already available within a school;

Students should first have experience with the various text forms and features before being expected to read or write similar forms.

1

- Providing guidelines for the acquisition of new material;
- Assisting teachers in planning and teaching more economically and intentionally;
- Identifying teaching points to help students understand the nature of a specific text form and how this affects the rate and style of reading or its function as a vehicle for written communication;
- Assisting teachers and students in establishing rubrics for planning and assessing writing and reading tasks and accomplishments;
- Identifying common targets within a school or grade level or group of classrooms.

Remembering What We Once Knew

It is hoped that this simple organization of once-familiar information will remind administrators and teachers of the nature and purpose of texts that we expect our students to read and write competently. There are many genre charts presenting different ways of categorizing a range of text forms. The contents of this book can be applied to most, if not all, such classifications. This book is based on three basic principles.

First, teachers need quick on-the-spot access to a host of information—prompts or nudges about the potential of a text, skill, or activity.

Second, if we want students to be able to read and write competently and independently, they need to understand the "why and how" and not just the "what."

Third, although there is no one sequence for any learning, all learning is dependent on what is already known. Learning is dependent on what has already been learned and this will affect all subsequent practice and learning.

Reassessing Material Already Available

Consideration of the questions at the end of the preface will remind readers that no series or collection of books, no matter how eclectic, will provide the breadth of material required to equal the gamut of reading and writing experienced in daily life. It is true that schools have a wealth of material, but much of it seems to remain on library shelves or be for the exclusive use of a grade level, standard of reader, teaching approach, or purpose. The majority of it is in book or magazine form and is intended for close or detailed reading. It is hoped that even a cursory examination of the range of text forms included in this book will prompt teachers and administrators to extend the range of material used for demonstrating, modeling, and instructional purposes, as well as for students' use for independent reading and writing.

> *No series or collection of books will provide the breadth of material required to equal the gamut of reading and writing experienced in daily life.*

It is possible that much of the material already available in a school may be underutilized. Students' attention may have been focused only on the story or the characters, plot, or setting, missing the empowering rewards of thinking a little deeper and considering how and why the author combined those elements and what supports or constraints the chosen text form offered. Many teachers have found it helpful to list some of the features of a book inside the front cover or on a bookmark, providing on-the-spot reminders for discussion or reflection. As other teachers use the book, more features are added or comments about most successful questions or follow-up activities are noted. If there are multiple copies of a title, one can be marked as the teachers' copy with a card attached to the storage box or the features noted on the box itself.

Many teachers using an earlier draft of this book listed titles of available books on self-stick labels or made notes in the margins of their copy, reminding them of material suitable for use with their students.

Providing Guidelines for the Acquisition of New Material

The word acquisition does not necessarily mean purchasing. Extending the range of material to provide a balance of text forms may require nothing more than collecting brochures, trade publications and documents, and other free material. However, as further purchases are planned, the listings in this book will help ensure adequate coverage for language and curriculum-specific programs at all grade levels.

Encouraging Economical and Intentional Teaching

The characteristics distinguishing one text form from another need to be understood from a reader and a writer's perspective. Knowing some of the features likely to be encountered enables the reader to consider the most appropriate reading style as well as make focused predictions about the content and the way it will probably be presented. In the same way, knowledge of the nature of a particular text type helps a writer compose and refine a piece of work according to the intended audience and purpose.

The following excerpts from a series of guided lessons with a fourth-grade class show how the teacher helped the students use and extend their knowledge of text forms and features to predict and confirm their style of reading as well as what was read.

> *Knowing some of the features enables the reader to consider the most appropriate reading style.*

What kind of book does this title lead you to expect?

Think about the biographies we have shared during the past week. Choose one that you particularly liked. Think about ways the author engaged your attention. What did she do to make you feel as if you really knew the person?

Think about the ways in which that biography was similar to others.

I will give you a few minutes to think about those things. You might like to make some notes ready for our group discussion.

The chart on the following two pages was created (Figure 1).

> *Presuming this author includes some of these features in this biography, how does this help you predict what kind of reader you will need to be?*
>
> *What information about the subject can you glean from the front cover and the blurb?*
>
> *Does the table of contents confirm that?*
>
> *What else does the table of contents tell you about this book or its subject?*
>
> *What do you hope to read about on the first few pages?*
>
> *Refer to our chart. What matches our list of probable features?*
>
> *What does that lead you to expect now?*
>
> *How did the book meet your expectations as a biography?*
>
> *Did you discover any more features common to biographies? Should these be added to the chart? If so, where? Are they linked with things already listed?*
>
> *When might you need to refer to the chart again?*
>
> *How would the chart help you next time you need to write some biographical notes or a biography?*
>
> *Look back at the chart we made when we read. . . biographies. Choose four or five features that you consider essential in a biography. Use that as a foundation for a rubric when you consider a piece of your writing.*

These excerpts show how students can be helped to think from a reader and a writer's perspective, providing meaningful follow-up activities that afford the teacher an opportunity to observe the degree to which each student is able to transfer the new understandings and skills. The chart used for predicting the reading also provides a framework for the prewriting and drafting stages. Similarly, it was used for reflecting on what was read and selecting elements for a rubric for students to evaluate their own writing.

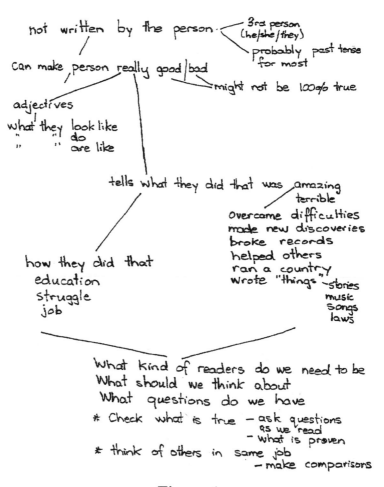

Figure 1

The following planning sheet has helped teachers make links between the various stages of reading and writing more overt. In the early grades, teachers use the sheets as reminders of elements within a book or skills currently being taught that are applicable to both reading and writing. In the upper grades, students can use the sheets when reading to record important features that may be useful in subsequent writing.

This planning sheet is provided as an example only (Figure 2). Teachers should develop materials that reflect their own under-

> • What we have learned
> 1. Authors need to do a lot of research
> 2. Authors use a lot of quotes and they
>   interview a lot of people – family
>   – descendants
>   – work mates
>   – friends
> 3. The photographs are grouped together
> 4. Some biographies do not have an index
> 5. 60% of our class like reading biographies
>   (That's 18)
>   Most of our class like biographies about
>   sports people and people who are alive
> 6. Biographies are not always books.
>   Magazines have biographies
>   (Some)   (called profiles)
>   (sometimes)
>
> What else we want to learn
>   Does the person in the book get paid
>   for having a book written about
>   them?
>   How long does it take to write a
>   biography?

Figure 1   continued.

standings and work for them and their learners. For instance, teachers may be more familiar with alternate phrases for some of the stages, such as "anticipating" for "predicting" and "attending" for "sampling" in the reading process and "planning" for "prewriting" and "proofreading" for "editing" in the writing process.

Identifying Teaching Points

The entries in the section on text forms and features do not in any way constitute a teaching sequence. It is not suggested that any student needs to learn all of the listed features of any one text. Teachers will need to select a few features, mindful that any one introduced will need revisiting, detailed explanation, and demonstration, supervised prac-

Reading	Writing
Predicting	Prewriting
Sampling	Drafting
Confirming	Revising
Self-correcting	Editing
Responding	Publishing
Reflecting and evaluating	Reflecting and evaluating

Figure 2

tice and application, and independent exploration and extension before becoming part of the student's repertoire of understandings and skills. Emphasis is also placed on a belief that a competent reader and writer's skill is dependent on the foundations laid at the earliest stage of development. What an emergent reader learns from and through reading a well-constructed book of a very low difficulty level affects their development at every subsequent stage as a reader, writer, and learner. Nothing should have to be unlearned—refined and extended, yes, but unlearned, no. Unlearning results in a loss of faith in the act of learning and in oneself. From the very earliest stages, students can be "taken behind the scenes" of a text they are reading and shown why and how texts are crafted, thus providing valuable information for their writing. For example, the following chart (Figure 3) provides a simple focus for predicting or framing lesson plans or scaffolding for the children as they read, compose, or evaluate some of the main text types.

Form	Probable main focus of content			
Narrative	Who	When	Where	What
Recount	When	What	Who	Where
Procedural	What	When	How	What if
Report	What	When	Who	Where
Expository	What	How	Why	Where

Figure 3

The following excerpts from a group of first-grade children reading *Night Walk*[1] demonstrate how knowledge of basic story structure can be a valuable predictive cue and a strong framework for writing.

Knowledge of basic story structure can be a valuable predictive cue and a strong framework for writing.

---

[1] Kenny, Ann. *Night Walk*. Katonah, New York: Richard C. Owen Publishers, Inc., 1996.

(Title: *Night Walk*. Illustration: Mother and child walking toward moon, cat following.)

Do you see any match between the cover illustration and the title?

Do you think this book is going to tell a story or give information?

If it is going to tell a story, which of our cards should we pull out?

(Children select "who," "when," "what," and "where" cards from a box containing multiples of what, when, why, who, how, where cards.

The box also contains larger cards marked in three rows labeled "beginning," "middle," and "end.")

Which cards go with the title? (what, when)

Which word tells what?

Which word tells when?

And which word goes with the illustration? (who)

Do we know where they walked? That might be something we found out in the story.

(Title page illustration: Cat looking through window at moon.)

I wonder why the cat is sitting here all alone.

> (page 3 text: Mama and I went for a walk to the store last night.)

What does the text tell you on page 3? (It tells who went for a walk, where they went, and when.)

Look at the cards. What do we need to know about now?

Think back to the illustration on the title page.

I wonder if. . .

Now turn to page 4.

(page 4 text: The cat followed us.)

Does that match what you predicted?

Do the pictures and text match?

A good story will probably have more than one incident.

Think about your favorite story. More than one thing happens, doesn't it? So what do you expect to see and read about on the next page?

(page 7 text: Our shadows followed us.)

Discussion after the reading included placing the small cards on the larger grid.

Let's look at the beginning of our story.

What did page 3 tell us?

Let's think of a story about . . . that tells us who and what and when.

A teacher may record these conversations (Figure 4).

My story tells:

- Who was there;
- What happened;
- Where it happened;
- When it happened.

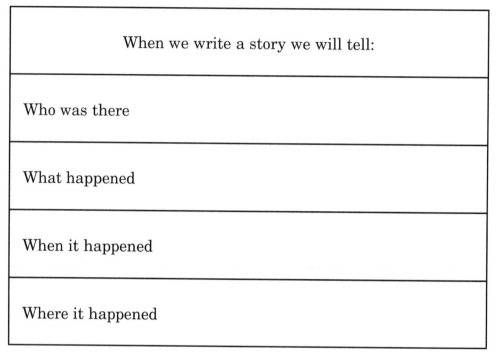

When we write a story we will tell:
Who was there
What happened
When it happened
Where it happened

Figure 4

Making Rubrics

The following example of a chart and rubric came from a first-grade class. After reading fables to and with the students and providing opportunities for the students to reread familiar fables and to independently explore new ones, the teacher helped the children identify five features as essential elements of fables.

The characters are always animals.

The animals act and talk likes humans.

There is always some trickery in the story.

A fable always has a moral. This is often at the end of the story.

Fables tell about one incident, so they can be classified as short stories.

	My mark	My teacher's mark
My characters are animals.		
The animals talk.		
My fable tells a moral.		

Figure 5

Each student then made a rubric (Figure 5) choosing three of these features to guide their planning and reflection when writing their own fables.

Identifying Common Targets

The competence and interest levels of any group of students and the features of a book will determine a suitable audience, the most appropriate teaching approach, and the teaching points. As already stated, any text form needs continuous revisiting. However, it is often a good idea for teachers of a grade level or combination of grade levels to identify a number of text forms that will probably provide a suitable focus for in-depth study. There will and should be overlap. Teachers of a similar grade can use the entries in this book to determine rubrics for marking tasks or assignments; for example, the common features will be emphasized as desirable in a science, social studies, or book report from a seventh-grade student.

Chapter 2

The Why and What of Each Text Form

Advertisements

Why

To develop loyalty to a cause, person, or product

To tantalize, persuade, and invite

To circularize information

To promote an event, product, cause, or person

To endorse a product over that of a competitor

To correct actual or perceived misinformation

To generate goodwill

To sell a service or product

What

Usually commercial presentation of information

Billboard, flier, circular, pamphlet, poster, packaging slip, banner, balloon, blurb

TV and radio spots, web site, insert or notice in magazines and newspapers, classified column, brochure (see separate entry), informational poster (see separate entry)

Features

Extensive use of graphics: layout, color, type font and size, visual images

Range of formats

Use concise language structures, often including colloquial terms or unconventional spelling

Persuasive language: superlatives, hyperboles, emotive adjectives, comparisons with competitors

Abbreviations and often abbreviated language; the latter are often specialized or technical terms

Often use metaphors, including clichéd metaphors, visual metaphors

Often include unsupported assertions, incomplete comparatives, or rhetorical questions

Often emphasize price, quality, reliability, new, or current product

Often designed to appeal to a specific audience or to extend audience

Sometimes include elements of urgency: limited availability, special offer, sale, discount

Frequently used vocabulary: trademark, retail price, guaranteed, warranty, special conditions apply, responsibility, sale, discount, limited, availability

Most include contact information: phone, fax, e-mail, web site, postal address

Radio and TV advertisements may include jingle or song

Printed advertisements will probably include a logo of the product or company

Excellence or superiority is often claimed rather than proven or backed by research

May include testimonies from anonymous people or from notable or public figures

Asterisk often refers to the "fine print" and the conditions or limitations or warnings

Order form or request for further information or for samples sometimes included

Size or duration of publication or distribution varies

Almost always linked to revenue

Conventional punctuation often omitted

May be supported through sponsorship—although not always indicated—in other cases the sponsorship is another form of advertising

Almanacs

Why

To provide information in a quick and easily accessible form

To show organization of the year or a period of time

To highlight specific dates or rhythms within a period

What

A book or table published annually containing information about events or topics connected with a specific group of people or activity

A book or table comprising a calendar of the year showing days, weeks, and months

A table showing the cycle of the sun and moon

A register or record of feast days

A record of astronomical or agricultural information

A record of genealogies and statistics

A book of reference material

Features

Layout consistent within document

Layout will vary according to purpose and origin (e.g., some weeks will begin on Monday, others Sunday)

Cultural influences determine the length and format of time periods

Often developed for a culture, religion, age group, or activity

Determine introduction or amendments of laws, taxes, or holidays

Information categorized by topic or chronologically or alphabetically organized

Often in column format

Usually include a range of visual text (e.g., tables, graphs, charts, diagrams)

Often include a range of typefaces and print sizes

Table of contents and index usually included

Atlases

Why

To show location, size, and some topographical features of a continent, country, or place within a country

To show location relative to other areas or within the world

What

A book of charts, diagrams, or graphs illustrating aspects of a place or subject

Collection of maps, each with a specific focus

Features

Maps may show outlines, topography, resources, or political divisions of regions, continents, the world, or galaxies

May have a very specific focus (e.g., an astronomical atlas)

Scale, key, legend

Abbreviations

Compass

Links or overlaps between maps

Introduction

Table of contents

Index with grid reference

Longitude and latitude

Symbols

Use of color or shading for relativity or to highlight features or location

Frequent revisions and editions

May include extra information (e.g., population, capital cities)

Range of typefaces or print sizes for emphasis or priority

Autobiographies

Why

To share achievements, influences, and incidents of one's life through the printed word

To correct misinformation

To reflect on one's own life

To acknowledge those who have made a contribution to the author's life

To explore a period of time

To justify actions

To provide insights into the attributes, personalities, interests, and opinions of the subject and of those close to the subject

To offer insights into the conditions and times in which the person lives/d

What

A first-person account (usually narrative) of all or part of one's life up to the time of writing

Diaries, memoirs, journals, personal letters, and annotated photographic albums are examples of autobiographical items

Features

Usually continuous narrative

Often unreliable as a record of facts

Disagreeable things often glossed over or omitted

May be based on memory or on other people's impressions and memories rather than research or reference to factual records

First person

Usually some emotive and reflective language

Usually includes feelings and opinions

Usually highlights one's better traits

May include flashbacks

Probably some direct and indirect speech

Index common

May have a ghost writer

Chapter headings usually descriptive

Illustrations most likely to be photographs, grouped and presented in signatures

Photographs usually grouped chronologically

Ballads

Why

To tell a story

What

A song that tells a story

A folk or traditional ballad or a literary ballad

Features

Folk ballads are usually passed on orally

Story is told through dialogue and action

Most begin with little scene setting and with a quick lead-up to
the crisis

Language is usually simple

Theme is often tragic

There is sometimes a refrain

Often only one episode

Biographies

Why

To chronicle a person's life

To highlight achievements

To dispel biased views

To publicize the subject

To perpetuate the memory of a person or achievements

To reflect on aspects of historical or topical interest

To acknowledge a person's influence on a group or cause

What

A written account of a person's life that focuses on character and career or achievements

An accurate history of a person's life or part of his or her life (as perceived at that time) and a reflection of the time and place in which he or she lived

Features

Detail may include family background, childhood experiences, education, personality traits, business ventures, comments by critics, contributions to his or her field of work or interest and the effects of these

Usually well researched

Research base may include diaries, newspaper clippings, official documents, subject's letters and memos to or from others, memories of contemporaries, personal knowledge

Illustrative material usually photographic

Photographs usually between signatures of book

Probably include quotes, anecdotes, or comments from other people

Usually shortcomings as well as virtues highlighted or at least included

Usually organized chronologically

May be written while subject still alive or posthumously

Chapter headings usually descriptive rather than numerical

If historical, may include genealogy chart

Adjectival, superlative, and comparative structures often included

Third person

May include footnotes and extensive bibliography

Book Reports

Why

To summarize reaction to a book

To influence other readers

To promote or introduce a book

What

A synopsis of a book, tailored for other potential readers, discussing noticeable features and new insights

Features

Differs from book review as a report focuses mainly on what is objectively observable

Format may be:

> title and author
>
> characters, setting, and point of view or purpose
>
> brief synopsis of content
>
> comment on the theme or perspective
>
> quotations from book to support statements
>
> recommendation on appropriate readership

Brochures

Why

To inform

To invite

To persuade

To market a product, attraction, or event

To create interest and goodwill

What

Single sheet, often folded, of promotional material advertising a
product, attraction, or event

Features

Symbols

Abbreviations

Directions

Schedules and timetables

Contact information: address, phone, fax, Internet

Language may vary within one brochure from concise and factual
(especially when giving information of price, responsibilities,
reservations) to emotive and persuasive descriptions using
superlatives and making comparisons with competitors

Persuasive language, often including superlatives or
unsubstantiated claims

Vocabulary: guarantee, reservations, responsibility, warranty,
location

Color, font, type size, and layout are important

Varied layout, sometimes confusing to reader

Illustrative material often assumes greatest emphasis and space

Illustrative material often includes photographs portraying best
aspects of subject and maps

Range from cheapest newsprint to glossiest art paper

Cartoons

Why

To entertain through satire or humor

To express an opinion

To persuade politically

What

A pictorial reflection on a topical issue, event, or person

An illustrative exaggeration of characteristics or issues

Features

Assume background knowledge

Captions or speech bubbles carry dialogue

Brief caption within frame gives time or setting

Inferential reading of illustrative material and caption required

Caricatures exaggerate peculiarities or defects, often for satiric effect

Often engender congenial rather than derisive laughter

Often topical and only of interest to specific group (e.g., local or where characters or issue are known)

Catalogues

Why

To provide information for quick retrieval

To uniquely identify a book, work of art, or product for ease of handling, tracking, or purchasing

To keep a record of books or works

What

An inventory of items, people, or events

A list, usually annotated, of books in a library or works in an exhibition for display or sale

A descriptive listing of items for sale

A classified listing of events

Trade publication

May be presented in card, brochure, or electronic form

Features

Usually include annotations or illustrations

May include price

Cataloging in Publication on the copyright page of a book provides classification information

Often includes abbreviated words or terms

Some are published regularly

Some are provided free and distributed widely

Classics

Why

Unlike other works, this label is not given by the author but is earned through long-lasting popularity

What

A work generally acknowledged as a model or example of a standard

A work of the highest class among others in similar form

A work that has been a long-standing favorite

Features

Usually several or many editions

Abridged versions common

Book language

Originals of older classics had few illustrations

What is perceived as a classic at one time might not be at another

Several works originally labeled as classics have been criticized for stereotyping

Cinquains

Why

To capture an image in a few descriptive words

What

A five-line stanza, usually unrhymed, with a set syllabic pattern

Features

Pattern of syllables: two, four, six, eight, two

Content usually related to nature

A single glimpse

Little or no connecting vocabulary

Comics

Why

To entertain through humor

To tell a story through pictures and minimal dialogue

What

A series of sequential framed illustrations with minimal text, mainly dialogue

A booklet or magazine containing one or more comic strips

Features

Action carried through illustration or dialogue

All text within frames

Dialogue and text describing setting or time minimal, usually caption within frame

Speech bubbles carry dialogue

Inferential reading required

Sequence of dialogue within frame often left to reader to decide

Characters often have their own series

Main distinction between issues is number and cover illustration rather than title

Contractions and idioms

Characters known through speech and action (no descriptive text)

Some comics have become classics

Consumer Reports

Why

To help potential buyers make an informed decision about a purchase

To maintain standards

To show how one product or service is viewed in relation to others available

To develop customer/client confidence

What

Specific type of trade publication

Evaluative surveys of goods and services for personal use

Objective presentation of advantages and disadvantages of a product or service in relation to others of similar intent

Features

Uses comparison and contrast and cause and effect

Rating system often present using numerals, stars, letters, percentages, or bar graphs

Usually prepared by independent group

Criteria known to readers

Field testing, clinical research, and/or consumer surveys

Often rated against national or international standards

Usually include summary and recommendations for purchase or use

Present and objective and impersonal tone

Use third-person point of view

Include headings, graphs, charts, tables

May include personal testimonies presenting positive or negative experiences

Usually include comments on value for money, performance rates, longevity, after sales service

Diaries

Why

To record events or thoughts day by day

Two distinct purposes—one as a planning record of appointments and the other as a reflective and personal record

For reflective reading or planning or scheduling

What

A book marked and arranged in calendar order in which to note appointments or keep a personal record of thoughts and activities

Features

Often part diary, part journal, and part notebook or memorandum

Arranged sequentially, day by day, and sometimes by shorter periods

Personal—often notes rather than complete sentences

Personal—emotive and descriptive language common

Personal—inner thoughts revealed

Appointments—usually only name and brief description of content

Abbreviations common

Personal diaries often for author's use only, sometimes written in or including codes

Appointment diary may be kept on behalf of someone else

Conventional punctuation and spelling often not important in personal diaries

Dictionaries

Why

To promote the correct or conventional use of language

To provide a common understanding of the meanings, use, and derivation of words

What

Reference book, arranged alphabetically, listing words and their meanings, alternative spellings, parts of speech, and often origins and pronunciation guides. Some dictionaries also use the word in a short sentence.

Reference book, arranged alphabetically, giving a word of similar meaning in another language

Reference book listing words for specific contexts or use—a biographical or mathematical dictionary, dictionary of synonyms and antonyms, rhyming dictionary

Features

Alphabetical listing with consistent format for each entry within style or edition

Parentheses

Abbreviations

Symbols

Pronunciation guide

Sounds and stress marks in pronunciation guide for each entry

Derivations of words

May include encyclopedic entries

Guide words as headers

Use of type for priority or function (bold, italics)

Variants, inflections, parts of speech, and grammatical information usually included

Directions

Why

To direct action

To give a sequence in order for something to be completed competently and successfully

To set out rules or parameters

What

Procedural texts giving step-by-step instructions

Sometimes a packaging slip or section of packaging

Features

Diagrams and figures are common

Layout is important, often with extra space between steps or each step framed

Sequence is critical and often numbered or indicated with ordinals or indicated by arrows, especially when diagrams carry main information or when layout is not uniform

Few adjectives

Each step often begins with imperative form of verb

Editorials

Why

To persuade others to have the same opinions as the editorial writer

To share opinions

To force public officials to reconsider decisions or priorities

To suggest alternative procedures

To influence readers

To bring current issues to the reader's attention

To entertain

What

A statement in a newspaper or magazine or on radio or TV that gives the opinion of the owner or delegated person

A short persuasive essay that expresses opinion or reaction to a news story or topical event

An informative outline of contents in a magazine

Features

Expresses opinion, often with overt bias

May be controversial

Anticipates counter arguments

Critical reading required for reader to make informed decision

Sometimes esoteric

Sometimes engenders emotive response from readers

May focus on the negative

Consistent placement and length

Usually written by chief editor

Encyclopedias

Why

To provide accessible reference material

To provide facts about a topic

What

A book, collection of volumes, or disk containing brief articles or information on various topics, often arranged alphabetically, dealing either with a range of knowledge or with a specific focus

Two main types: specialized or comprehensive

Features

Usually updated regularly, hence editions are important

Often presented in volumes

Often multiple writers, including people eminent in their profession or anonymous contributors

Preface to each edition noting reason for or summary of changes

Usually includes some illustrative material

Carefully researched

Usually objective with little or no bias

Detailed index with key reference usually in bold

Abbreviations

Often in columns with guide words

Epics

Why

To present models of greatness of character

To record heroic deeds

To reflect the history and values of a culture

To comment on a social issue of the period

To rally patriotism

What

A long narrative story or poem set in a remote time and place and about a heroic character/characters and heroic deeds, misadventures, or perilous journeys

Features

Characters larger than life in strength, intellect, and/or bravery

Content important in history of a nation

Character reflects full range of virtues of the time

Many originally written in poetic form

Strong supernatural element

Translations may lose rhythm and strength of emotion, bravery, or danger of original

Many of the originals were sung or spoken to the accompaniment of a musical instrument

Danger and a battle of physical strength common essential elements

Essays

Why

To explain, explore, or argue ideas on a single topic

To entertain through discussion of an idea or opinion

What

A composition on a theme or topic

A short, nonexhaustive composition in which ideas on a single topic are explained or argued in an interesting manner

A brief exploratory composition rather than an authoritative or comprehensive dissertation

Formal essay, informal essay, biographical essay, photo essay, narrative essay, response to questions

Features

Nearly always written in prose (note: photo essays)

Maintains tight focus on topic

Most essays are relatively short

Follow clear organizational form

Directed toward a specific audience

May include elements of humor, pathos, or exaggeration

May include cause and effect, analogies, opinion, persuasion, classification, descriptions, reviews, comparison, and contrast

Introductory sentence presents issue and perspective

Expository Texts

Why

To explain the what, when, why, or how of facts, ideas, and opinions

To explain an idea, develop a thought, and prove a point or fact

What

Explanatory writing, detailing or justifying information, ideas, and opinions

In short form: essay, article

In longer form: travel book, research paper, informational text

Features

Usually nonfiction

Tells how, where, when, why, which things happen or have happened or are as they are

Tells:

> what things are like—size, color, shape, texture
>
> what things can do—movement, use
>
> how many
>
> where things are found

Usually detailed and descriptive

Information organized logically

Systematic explanations or arguments

Often includes illustrative material, especially diagrams and tables

Longer expository texts usually have a table of contents and index and descriptive headings

Many have a bibliography

Detailed reading is usually required

Fables

Why

To demonstrate a moral

What

A short and fairly simple didactic story in prose or verse, usually with animal characters acting as humans

A traditional form of story related to proverbs and folklore

Features

Characters in literary fables are anthropomorphic

Characters are impersonal—called by generic name

Characters represent aspects of human nature, e.g., sheep represents innocence

Animal characteristics often exhibit human frailties

Usually one, two, or three characters

Element of trickery as turning point

Usually one incident

More complex than often thought—conveying abstract truth in very few words

Fantasy

Why

To transport the reader into an imaginary world

To provide enjoyment

To encourage the reader to think beyond the realms of reality

To present a satirical view of an event or system

What

Term for writing not anchored in reality

Includes science fiction, fables, folk and fairy tales

Writing set in imaginary circumstances detailing events that push principles of science and physics

Features

Reader often left with no explanation for strange events or behavior

Characters often have surreal powers

May include "utopic" elements of an ideal society or political system

Credibility often gained through detailed description or similes with everyday items or events

Feature Articles

Why

To provide information of human interest

To evoke an emotional response

To provide another view or more detail to topical issues or events

To introduce a forthcoming event

To highlight an achievement

What

An article, usually in a magazine or newspaper, placing emphasis on people or social issues rather than facts or news

Features

Do not necessarily follow structure of regular/news article—may be based on importance, flashbacks, sequence, or be a descriptive character sketch

Should be well researched

Title and/or introductory sentence designed to capture reader's curiosity and emotion

Concluding section should tie loose ends together and provide finality without summarizing text

Writing should have an air of originality and crispness

Folk Tales

Why

To tell an entertaining story

To reveal human nature

To instill cultural beliefs, values, and practices

To explain natural and social phenomena

To kindle imagination

To discover universal qualities of humankind

What

Forms of narrative that have been handed down, usually orally

Epic, fairy tale, ballad, myth, legend, fable, folk song, tall story, shaggy dog story, ghost story, short humorous tale often about local "colorful" characters

Features

May not have been intended for children, but strong plot, quick action, and identifiable structure have attracted children through the ages and across cultures

Usually reasonably short

Almost always end happily

The "underdog" usually triumphs or good overcomes evil

Wishes come true as a result of a test or struggle

Element of magic, often magical transformation at resolution point

Every culture has its own folklore reflecting its history and values

Identifiable structure

Action quickly reflects direct plot

Characters, setting, and problem revealed early

Characters often opposite in character and appearance—usually several adjectives to describe each character

Quick ending contains resolution—sudden demise of antagonist; instant, painless, and bloodless death; lavish wedding without apparent preparation

Repetition a basic element—repetition often related to number of characters, especially three

Three is a common element—characters, main episodes, attempts to solve problems

Chants or repeated verses are common

Always set in distant past

Many versions of same tale—often adapted to a culture but also many versions within a culture

The same theme is reflected in different tales in different cultures

Haiku

Why

To capture a single impression of a scene or natural object

What

A lyrical poem of Japanese origin with a definite structure that focuses on a single moment

A "miniature snap" in words

Features

English: seventeen syllables arranged in three lines of five, seven, and five syllables

Creates clear images

Written in present tense

Focuses on natural object or scene

First part focuses on some aspect of nature and the second on the engendered mood or emotion

Often relates to seasons or to time of day

Evokes emotion

Readers needs to add context and often create the setting

Often includes alliteration and/or onomatopoeia

Informational Posters

Why

To convey a large amount of information in a succinct and
graphical form to a distant and fleeting audience

What

Billboard, flier, TV advertisement, wall chart

Features

Appeal to a specific audience

May include slogan, logos, reference to public figures

Illustrations may include photographs of well-known people

Link with product may be obscure but causes tend to be overtly
explicit

Graphics, color, and layout usually sell the message

Inferential reading a common requirement

Use concise language

Often include metaphors

Interviews

Why

To record conversations with or questioning of a person for a
specific purpose or audience

To obtain and share information about predetermined topics
through a question and answer session

What

Usually magazine or newspaper article set out in question and
answer format

Features

Little or no scene setting

Verbatim recording of questions and answers

Interviewee does not usually have opportunity to use reference
material

Use of bold type, abbreviations, and colons in presentation

May include idioms, incomplete structures

Usually involves some preparation on part of the interviewer—
research on subject, questions to initiate discussion or elicit or
support a bias

Sidetracking is common

May include "supporting" elements, including photographs, scene-
setting introduction, editor's note, film clips, footnotes

Journals

Why

To provide a record of thoughts, experiences, dreams, memories, plans

What

A scholarly periodical

A personal record of thoughts, impressions, and events important for the present or as a plan for future reference or action

Can be a form of diary

Features

Entries dated, often on a daily basis

Include summaries, responses, unanswered questions

Contain autobiographical information

First person

May be a mixture of tenses

Often focuses on what has been learned

Can be a source of ideas for writing or some action

Entries may be more sporadic than in diaries

Entries may be more reflective of thoughts, impressions, and ideas than in a diary

Legends

Why

To explain a social phenomena

To focus on positive character traits

To present models of behavior and ethics

To use story to explain aspects of human nature

What

Narrative, often part fact and part fiction, about the life and deeds of a famous hero or a saint, kept alive mainly through oral retellings

Story about heroes before the time of recorded history

Features

Focuses on character traits, especially of strength and bravery

Often exaggerated accounts—some of the acts of heroism become more exaggerated with each retelling

Many have historical basis

Many follow the pattern of traditional tales

Often called hero myths

Often distinguished from myths in that they have humans rather than gods as characters and they sometimes have a historical basis that myths do not have

Many epics are based on legends

Letters, Business

Why

To request or to respond to a request

To express an opinion

To inform

To apply for a product, information, or a position

To establish correspondence, usually with someone in another place

What

Correspondence related to profession or to business matters of ·personal life

Correspondence between two parties, one of whom is part of an organized body

Features

Layout more detailed and body of letter has more defined structure than that of a personal letter

Full address of sender and recipient included along with full contact details

Often on letterhead

Structure includes purpose of letter and reference to any previous correspondence on the same topic, explanation, and thanks that often summarizes intended or decided action.

Clear, precise writing addressing point or points with few pleasantries

Follow standard grammar, spelling, and usage

Opinion often stated as fact

May include: Reference:, Attention:, our reference:, a subject line, postscript

Recipient or writer may be acting on behalf of a group or
   committee

May be more than one recipient, denoted by "cc"

May include technical information specific to topic or specific item

If more than one item is being discussed, paragraphs

Might be numbered with subsection defined by letters

Copy kept by sender

Enclosure(s) indicated at bottom of letter

Letters, Editorial

Why

To express an opinion to a wide audience

To correct misinformation or add further information to an article, previous letter, or an issue or event

What

Letter addressing a timely subject intended for wide and public readership

Letter of opinion in a regular column within a newspaper or magazine

Features

Written by member of the public or one of the readers

May be written on behalf of a group of people

Only selected letters are published

Letter may be abridged for publication

Opinions are expressed early within letter

Full contact details or addresses are seldom included, requiring continuing correspondence to be through the newspaper or magazine

Letters, Personal

Why

To maintain a relationship

To exchange records of incidents and ideas of common interest

To extend, accept, or decline an invitation

To offer congratulations or condolences

What

A written communication from one person to another, traditionally sent in an envelope by post, but electronic mail is becoming more common

Often referred to as friendly letters

Features

Greetings and signatures are usually by first name

Sequence may not be important

Idioms and natural language are common elements

Often include flashbacks, references to common experiences or ideals, plans, or opinions of events or people

Some content probably of significance only to writer and main recipient

Often used in research for biographies or autobiographies

Address and date often abbreviated

Usually longer than business or functional letters

Grammar and spelling are not as closely checked as in other forms of letters

Limericks

Why

To entertain

To sell a product or service

What

A five-line light or nonsense verse in which the first, second, and fifth lines rhyme, as do the third and fourth

Features

Lines one, two, and five have three stresses, while the third and fourth lines have two

Sometimes the third and fourth lines are combined, creating internal rhyme within a four-line verse

Final line often presents a witty turn on the subject

Last word of fifth line sometimes repeats final word from first

Sometimes adapted to a popular tune and sung as an advertisement

Lists

Why

To provide quick access to information with a common purpose or focus

To provide a quick reference for considering ideas or facts and their relationships

To plan or to outline intended action

What

A collection, often arranged vertically, of words or phrases with a common theme

Features

Often the result of individual or collective brainstorming

Usually same parts of speech within a list

May be reorganized into a logical sequence to form an outline or procedure

May include bullets or numbering

May focus on main ideas

Can be a form of note taking or planning

Magazines

Why

To provide short reads on a variety of subjects or different aspects or views of a single topic or theme within one publication

To pursue a topic or issue on a regular basis

To update information

To inform readers of the lives of famous people

To provide the views of several people

To develop loyalty to a product or cause

What

A periodical associated with a specific group or topic

A collection of items published for a specific audience or to promote a cause

A volume or issue with a consistent format and approach

Features

Light and easy to handle

Often free or inexpensive

Some sustained by subscription or copies sold or revenue from advertisements

Offer detailed reading or content for "dipping and delving"

May be biased or emphasize a perspective

Each issue may vary according to focus and contributors

Cover gives information of main topics or the focus

Usually wide range of graphics within an issue

Columns

Variety of type

Technical or specialized vocabulary

Items may be continued from one issue to another

Color, illustrative material and graphics, and layout are important elements in most

Contents may include:

      cover information—publication date, issue, volume, key topics, or theme

      table of contents

      publication staff

      publication information

      subscription information

      editorial

      reviews

      letters to the editor

      profiles

      feature articles

      articles

      advertisements

      achievements and milestones

      forthcoming events or issues

      latest news or research

      interviews

      regular features (puzzles, recipes, snippets, reports)

Magazine Articles

Why

To explain, inform, express opinion, report

To engender interest or response

What

Item within a collection

Often a stand-alone item within the collection, either by form or content

Features

Usually topical or current and linked to focus of magazine

May be by regular contributor to magazine

May be a topic of short-term or immediate interest

Often biased

Manuals

Why

To guide or direct action

To explain the components and/or operation of a product

To explain how materials or equipment can be used or repaired

What

An intermediary between manufacturer and consumer

A procedural text

A factual and descriptive explanation of how, what, when, and why

Also referred to as handbook

Features

Usually includes technical or specialized language

Diagrams are usually labeled and referenced from text

Diagrams often show sequence, are cut away to show inner components, or just label components

Requires detailed reading, though tendency is often to skim or refer to diagrams first

Often uses bold or italic type and framed sections

Chapter summaries often in note form at beginning of chapter

Detailed index and often a troubleshooting section

Often subsections within table of contents

Appendices may include specifications

Authorized service agents

May include safety warnings and warranties

Memoirs

Why

To record thoughts or actions for future reference or reflection

What

Form of autobiography

Usually focuses on a single period in author's life and on notable
people known to author

May be selected from longer or more detailed recordings of events
and thoughts

Features

First person

Narrative

May be selected diary or journal entries or letters to a close friend
or family member or selections from official documents

Usually focus on a period of time reflecting on the implications of
a major event in the author's life or a specific historical period

Usually little illustrative material

Often very descriptive, with attention to detail of places or
emotions

Sometimes strong characterization of third party through detailed
description of actions, speech, or physical attributes

action or to direct action

s on a project or request

ote, or written message, usually

branches of a business, of something

mbered or accomplished

Fea

Headings include: To, From, Date, Subject, and others receiving a copy for information (might be listed as "cc")

Formal memos are often copied to superior of both writer and recipient

May be more than one recipient, denoted by "cc"

May be reporting on conversations or reminding of agreed action

Printed form or e-mail may determine format

Usually written like a business letter with main idea in first paragraph followed by necessary details and indication of required response or action

Copy kept by sender

Often includes file reference

Language may include imperatives

Minutes

Why

To provide a record of the official business of a meeting

What

A secretary's documentation of decisions, reports, queries, recommendations, financial matters, and intended action discussed at a meeting of people with a similar interest or duty

Features

Consistent format that includes:

> date, time, and place of meeting
>
> name of person who calls meeting to order
>
> list or number of those present
>
> list or number of absent members
>
> indication of reading and acceptance or amendment of minutes of previous meeting
>
> listing and/or summary of committee reports and actions
>
> list of unfinished business
>
> record of new appointments
>
> explanation of any business transacted, including names of proposer and seconder of motions, and any actions taken
>
> list of forthcoming events or business
>
> date, time, and place of next meeting
>
> time of adjournment
>
> secretary's signature

Written by secretary

Read at next meeting for endorsement

Agenda of meeting forms skeleton of minutes

Motions are recorded word for word, along with proposer's and seconder's names

Sometimes circulated beyond those present at meeting, especially minutes of a committee meeting made available for general members

Myths

Why

To explain how something came to exist

To explain aspects of life, culture, and nature

To explain origins

What

In some cultures and religions and in a literary sense "myth" does
not mean untrue but a generalized understanding or belief

An anonymous narrative that explains the origins of life and
elements of nature

A fictional story containing a deeper truth

A fictional story that involves supernatural beings

A fictitious tale kept alive mainly through oral tradition

Features

Characters are supernatural beings or elements of nature
personified

Many follow the pattern of traditional stories

Short stories that contain action and suspense

Every culture has its own collection of myths as well as a
universal bank of myths

Each culture has its own creation and nature myths—the former
about how the world began, the sun and moon got in the sky
and the latter explaining seasonal changes, movements of the
sun and earth, animal characteristics

Preserved mainly through oral tradition, especially in earlier
times

Narratives

Why

To entertain

To enable the reader to enjoy experiences vicariously

To record experiences

What

The record of a series of factual or fictional events in which the linking of the events gives a sequence and shape to the telling

Short stories, epics, ballads, biographies, autobiographies, novels, romances are examples of narratives

Features

Realistic, humorous, fantasy, historical, science fiction

Structures familiar in narratives for beginning readers include cumulative, interlocking or chain (ab, bc, cd, . . .), common sequences (seasons, days of the week), rhyme, repetition, and time sequence

Has a theme rather than a topic

An identifiable problem or tension that gives shape to the plot:

beginning—introduction of characters, setting, problem

middle—development and elaboration of problem or tension, introduction of other elements

conclusion—resolution or acceptance of inevitable

Characters, mood, tension, strength of story line, and setting are interwoven and interdependent elements

Often rely on sensory details for impact

Usually include description and dialogue

Relies on sensory details for impact

Newspapers

Why

To inform readers of international, national, and local events, services, and opportunities

What

A collection of topical news reports, articles, notices, and advertisements, published daily or weekly, on folded sheets of paper

Features

May have a specific focus or bias

Main components:

> articles
>
> reports
>
> editorial
>
> advertisements
>
> classified advertisements
>
> public notices
>
> personal messages
>
> obituaries
>
> classified index
>
> special features

Subsections may include:

> entertainment opportunities
>
> deaths, births, and marriages
>
> houses, land, vehicles, products for sale
>
> employment opportunities
>
> financial and transport information
>
> tourism information
>
> reports of meetings

legislation

sports

Larger newspapers divided into regular sections, many with a daily feature section

Layout consistent from one issue to another

Some newspapers in large cities may have more than one edition per day

Layout usually in columns with headlines often spreading across columns

Majority of each paper, and all of some, are in black and white on newsprint paper

Usually have regular readership; home delivery still common

Preparation time for each issue is very short, usually less than 24-hour turnaround, giving sense of urgency for staff and immediacy for reader

Many people will work on one item in a short time prior to publication, including reporter, editor, subeditor, typesetter, proofreader, designer

Variety of typefaces and sizes within one issue

Newspaper Articles

Why

To provide information or opinion about a current topic or issue

What

Two main categories: news article that provides a record of what happened or what was said, and a feature article that offers opinion or focuses on the human aspect

Features

News articles usually written by journalists or publicity personnel for an organization or business

Key or topic sentence is important because editing for space limitations may cut some of the subsequent details or explanations

Includes who, what, where, when, why, and how

Details are added in order of importance

News articles should report events factually and objectively, whereas feature articles often include opinion, judgment, and assumptions

Follow standard rules of grammar, punctuation, and format

Feature articles usually include background information

Novels

Why

To entertain

To cause reflection on one's own life

To live vicariously

To provoke emotion

To encourage thought

What

A lengthy fictional narrative in prose presenting incidents, characters, and a setting shaped in a sequence or plot

Detective story, romantic novel, historical novel, science fiction, contemporary story, chronicles, sagas

Features

Although the work is fictional, the author presents the characters, incidents, and settings as realistically as possible

Most widely read form of literature

Usually long enough to be a publication by itself, although length varies greatly—widely accepted to be between 60,000 and 200,000 words

Relationships and their changing nature are usually essential elements in a novel

Characters imitate those found in real life

Usually no table of contents

Chapter headings usually numbered rather than titled

Plot is presented through thought, action, speech of characters

Each type of novel has its own features, for example, in historical novels:

> setting gains greater importance—clothing, transport, social protocol, houses must all reflect time and place
>
> dialogue may include unusual structures or phrases, or words may have a different meaning, requiring the reader to make greater use of context and perhaps use read-on strategies
>
> may require extra background knowledge or extra attention to detail if reading is not to be interrupted researching
>
> usually past tense—if not, the reader will have to remember setting and time to cope with actions and dialogue

Novelette

Why

To entertain

To capture a short period of time

What

Also called a novella

A long short story in narrative form presenting a single event or conflict with a surprise element signaling the turning point

A work of fiction longer than a short story but shorter than a novel

Often used negatively to describe sentimental romances, stories, or thrillers

Features

Development of character and theme important

Parables

Why

To teach a lesson through something or someone's experiences

To present an abstract idea through credible and everyday situations

What

A short and simple story with a moral

An allegory that parallels the situation to which it is being applied

Features

Action and consequence are key to the form

Comparisons between characters are usually important

Usually more than one incident

Moral may be presented in character's dialogue or thought at end of parable or left for reader to determine

Plays

Why

To entertain

To provoke thought and emotion

To present a visual and aural experience for the audience and a
participatory one for the players

What

A dramatic work written in dialogue for presentation by one or
more players

Usually consist of two parts: spoken dialogue portion and
directions to enhance the spoken portion

Tragedy, comedy, tragi-comedy, black comedy, burlesque, satiric
comedy, farce, mystery, melodrama, pantomime, musicals,
operas

Features

Directions describe setting, lighting, movement of characters and
props, intonation of dialogue, costumes

Characters usually include at least one protagonist and antagonist

Characters listed at beginning, usually in order of appearance

Character listing usually includes very brief description of age,
appearance, role in play, or relationship to other characters

Action is vital with rising elements, crises, climax, and falling
action

Plots moves through showing rather than telling

May include a soliloquy

May include flashbacks

Major division of longer plays is acts divided into scenes

Setting for each scene is given in italics at beginning of text for
scene

Stage directions usually in italics and square brackets at appropriate place in script, set in middle of page

Stage directions begin with a capital letter and end with a period or full stop even if not complete sentence

Lines and sections are sometimes numbered on left-hand side of page as a reference aid

Hanging indentation offsets speaker's name

Within dialogue, character's name usually in bold even capitals

Poems

Why

To create images through the rhyme and rhythm of language

To express thoughts and feelings through lyrical language

To cause reflection on the essence of an object, thought, observation, or experience

To broaden or intensify the reader's experiences and understandings

What

Language composed according to a pattern of beat and melody of words

A work of verse, which may be in rhyme or in blank verse or a combination of the two, in which the words are linked and interdependent through sense and rhythm

Three main categories of poems—narrative, dramatic, and lyrical—and many subcategories within each

Many forms including ballad, blank verse, epic, dramatic monologue, elegy, epigram, free verse, sonnet, limerick, ode, haiku

Features

Vary in length from a few lines to book-length epics

Every word is chosen for its sound as well as meaning and function

Meter and rhythm, and sometimes rhyme, determines line length

Rely on imagery to stimulate reader's thought and view of a larger message

The images created by the syntax, rhythm, and context bring a poem to life

Usually more condensed than prose or everyday speech

Frequent and elaborate use of figures of speech, especially similes and metaphors or techniques for comparing and contrasting

Every culture has its own poetry and it is often associated with rituals or festivities or seasonal activities

Often focus on intensity of emotion or observation

Often depart from usual word order or pronunciation or uses archaic words or creates new ones

Much of the meaning is conveyed by suggestion or by omission

Often include words with multiple meanings, making every word count more than once

Reader needs to read and think beyond the superficial

Difficult to paraphrase

Sometimes the rhythm of the language and the pattern of the lines reflect the mood of the content

Alliteration and assonance may complement or even replace the rhyme

Repetition is a common element—repetition of sounds, words, lines, phrases, and images

Layout is important and often controls the pace and style of reading

Usually past or present tense

Often in first person or character anonymous

Uses unconventional punctuation and line breaks to convey meaning or to show relationships between ideas

Policies

Why

To set parameters

To ensure consistency

To make expectations and standards known

To maintain standards or ideals

To safeguard integrity or processes

What

Contractual documents outlining responsibilities of all involved
parties and the conditions under which the responsibilities
are to be executed

Features

Document outlines expected outcomes and ways in which these
will be achieved

Headings and subheadings and clauses and subclauses

Signatures of main parties or a representative of each

Usually a time limit for the life of a policy

Usually checked by a legal adviser

Signatures usually need to be witnessed by an objective party

Formal language

May include procedures for revision

May include penalty or cancellation clauses

Vocabulary: indemnify, subsidiary rights, contractual,
infringement, royalties

Procedural Texts

Why

To direct thought or action

To give a sequence for an action

What

A detailed sequence of how and when to do or say something in order to achieve a planned result

Recipes, instructions, manuals, blueprints, rules, handbooks, directions, laws

Features

Vocabulary: ingredients, method, procedure, "ordinals," assemble, construct, join, materials, equipment

Present or future tense

Second or third person

Indirect speech

Usually short sentences

Numbering, bullets, or arrows

Each step may start on a new line

May include diagrams (cutaway, outline, shaded are focusing on current action) or figures with insets for more detail of specific parts

Composite diagram showing or summarizing several steps

Explanatory captions

May include troubleshooting section

Prose

Why

To entertain

To inform

To express

To persuade

To create thought

To imitate life

What

Straightforward oral or written discourse—the language of short stories, essays, and novels

Continuous text usually read from left to right and top to bottom

Features

Straight prose is not restricted by rhyme or rhythm, although there is poetic prose or a prose poem

Not organized according to a formal pattern

Continuity of thought is important

Paragraphs and chapters are the main divisions in prose

Punctuation is used conventionally

Length and complexity of sentence as well as word choice and author's style determine how effectively the content is conveyed

Proverbs

Why

To encapsulate a major idea within a few words

To present a commonplace truth or a useful thought

What

An ancient and wise saying, usually of unknown origin

A truth based on common sense

Features

Succinct but didactic

Often linked to common happenings

Often handed down through oral tradition

Public Documents

Why

To inform the public of existing regulations and of deletions, additions, or amendments

To invite discussion on matters of public interest

To inform a wide audience on a matter of community action or interest

What

Publications issued by national, state, and local governments and agencies: journals, debates, acts, hearings, reports, committee documents, census data

Features

Publications are issued by Congress and state Senates and Houses of Representatives, executive departments, agencies, local authorities, courts, regional departments

Many public documents are numbered with year and a serial number (if legislation, will usually also include session number)—important because of frequent amendments or a change in status

Legal and formal language

Copyright usually belongs to governing body, even if written by an individual

Most are printed and distributed free by government agency

Clauses and subclauses

House and Senate journals published at the end of each session containing motions, actions taken, and votes on roll calls

Reports and other public documents of frequent publication may be bound in serial sets

Recounts

Why

To give a sequential and detailed account of an incident, a series of incidents, or a conversation

What

A written record of recall of events, with attention to sequence and accuracy, and often to detail

Features

Indicators in children's books include days of the week, use of ordinal numbers, characters acting in sequence, cumulative structures

Past tense

Sequence and time are important

Vocabulary: then, next, first, after that, immediately following, prior to, followed by

Dialogue and/or indirect speech may be interspersed throughout

May be presented with author's or observer's opinions as an introduction or closing or as asides

No flashbacks

Reports

Why

To record research, decisions, or events

To keep a record of progress on a task

To present information to inform or to persuade

What

A written summary of one or a series of incidents, conversations, studies, or observations

Newspaper and magazine articles, research papers, biographies, travel books, consumer reports, minutes of meetings, diaries, journals, some realistic fiction

Features

Includes some prioritizing, summarizing, generalizing, and paraphrasing

Purpose and subject established in introductory statement

Often includes a statement on how the information was gathered

More indirect than direct speech, but may include quotes

Past tense

Organization may be chronological or topical

May include numbering, subheadings, margin entries, bullets, and asterisks

May include references

Some reports include recommendations

Framework for a nonfiction report:

      introduction

      terms of reference

      background information

      facts

opinions
conclusions
recommendations
summary (in some cases, this may come at the beginning)
bibliography

Reports, Technical

Why

To present facts clearly and objectively

To show how to solve a problem

To show results of a study or survey

To explain the operation of a machine or program

To detail procedures and findings

To summarize processes

What

An objective recording or summary of processes and procedures associated with a specific profession, procedure, or piece of equipment

Features

Does not include personal opinion

Usually include vocabulary specific to the subject

Often include specifications

Written in impersonal voice

Usually formatted by headings

Often include graphs, diagrams, comparative tables

Have table of contents and cite all references

May include an appendix containing more detailed statistics or information than in body of text

Usually include comparisons

Research Papers

Why

To report or to evaluate research findings

What

A summary of the intent, process, sequence, and content of the research, provable findings, and conclusions

Features

Introduction establishes a thesis to be developed

May include direct quotations, paraphrases, or précis that support the thesis

May include endnotes, footnotes, or parenthetical notes

Includes a list of works cited

Should include reference to other research on the same topic, especially if issue is controversial

An abstract usually introduces the thesis and is a single paragraph, without indentation

A summary statement includes conclusions of findings and perhaps the implications of these

Rhymes

Why

To create images

Emphasizes similarity between sounds

Emphasizes the musical quality of rhythmic and rhyming language

To provide a beat or rhythm for everyday chores

What

A verse or piece of poetry with corresponding sounds at the ends of the lines

A short verse or poem with a strong repetitive rhythm and emphatic rhyme

Counting, playground, skipping, or nursery rhymes; jingles, nonsense rhymes, limericks, chants

Features

Normally the last stressed vowel in the line and all sounds following it make up the rhyming element

Many survive because of the rhythm rather than the meaning, which is often irrelevant outside original context

Many are part of oral tradition of a culture

Origins of most traditional rhymes are obscure

Many are based on proverbs, riddles, street cries, chants from stories

Often humorous

Schedules

Why

To inform readers of sequence and timing of items, actions, or
events

To inform workers of tasks and timing for each

To show the interdependence of the work of members of a team

To provide information, often comparative, in a concise format

What

A plan or procedure to achieve a specific objective including the
sequence of and time allotted for each particular section of
work and whose responsibility it is to perform and check each
task

A detailed planning timeline

A list of predetermined and nonnegotiable information, such as
times or prices

Features

Usually presented in tabular form

Often based on time

Sometimes forms an appendix to a more descriptive or a more
general document

May be updated frequently

Any change usually has a domino effect

Science Fiction

Why

To suggest hypotheses about improbable or impossible transformations about aspects of human existence

To encourage readers to view the world from a different perspective

To develop imagination and flexible thought

What

A form of fiction that makes use of scientific knowledge and/or conjecture

Features

Usually prose but also science fiction comics

Form of literary fantasy

Setting, plots, themes, and characters are based on scientific or technological speculation

Writer has to construct a futuristic world in which certain unknowns are accepted as proven fact

Setting and characters have to be believable and credible down to the last detail

Reader is put into a "what if" mode of thinking

Assumes a world vastly different from the one we know

Common elements are humans projected onto another planet, a creature from another planet visiting earth, life on earth after a major ecological disaster, humans transported into a futuristic world, one human among a group of aliens

Often raises questions of ethics or causes reader to think of enduring human qualities and responsibilities

May include preface or introduction that gives some information about setting or origin of characters

Songs

Why

To entertain

To combine words, tune, and rhythm in a planned sequence

What

A piece of music with text for the voice

A poem and its musical setting (although some poems are called songs, even if not set to music); a poem for singing or chanting

Ballad, war song, chant, aria, madrigal, lyric, hymn

Features

Music and words may be composed together or one after the other

Document outlined expected outcomes and ways in which these will be achieved

Verse often equivalent of stanza

Imagery, figures of speech, rhyme, and alliteration are common elements

Sonnets

Why

To express love or passion

To highlight the significance of an event

To portray an element of nature

To express religious understandings

What

A fourteen-line poem, either in an eight-line octave and six-line sestet (Italian) or in three quatrains and a final couplet (English)

Features

Lines of equal length

The eight- and six-line form usually develops an idea in eight lines and then creates a turn or different perspective for the final six. The other form introduces the topic in the first quatrain, develops it in the next two, and concludes with a summarizing couplet

Sometimes a group of sonnets is linked to form a longer work or "sonnet sequence" or a "novel"

Often express love or feelings about a person or event, inner thoughts about one's hopes, or thoughts about life and death

Speeches

Why

To influence the audience to support a cause or to understand the speaker's perspective

To justify actual or proposed action

To inform audience of views, news, or facts or a combination of these

What

A talk or an address delivered to an audience

Features

Organization of ideas and facts must have a logical sequence because listeners do not usually have a printed reference

Basic format is introduction, statement of the case, which may include points to be made or position taken, argument or explanation of position, conclusion

May include some visuals

Rhetorical questions, personal experiences, or humorous anecdotes often interspersed through main content to emphasize a point, engender emotive reaction, or maintain interest

May include some informal language or idioms

Short sentences to enable reader to maintain focus

Summaries

Why

To present a shortened version of a piece of work

To identify the main ideas or information in a longer work

To make the original work more accessible to a specific audience

To clarify ideas or information

To provide quick access to main ideas or those pertinent to an aspect of the original topic or theme

To note main or specific ideas or information for later reference

What

There are three main types of summaries:

> précis—shortened restatement of main ideas of original, without personal bias
>
> paraphrase—restates original work in own words
>
> synopsis—states reader's view of main ideas

Features

Depends on reader's understanding of original work

Synopsis and paraphrase reflect style of reader/current writer

Paraphrase may not reduce length as much as other two forms of summaries

May include key words and selected phrases or short quotations from original

Paraphrases should reduce technical or complicated writing to a simpler style

Précis should maintain same organization as original

Supportive or illustrative material is omitted from a précis or synopsis

Tall Tales

Why

To record an exaggerated version of a real or imaginary heroic or humorous act

What

A humorous account of adventures popular on the nineteenth century American frontier

Folk tales specific to a culture and to pioneering feats

Features

Often exaggerated tales

Usually involves superhuman feats

Similar in structure to a folk tale

Focus on the pioneer spirit required to adapt to harsh environment

Superlatives common

Trickery

Problems or tussles often solved with good humor

Some are based on real characters, often with invented or exaggerated incidents and traits

Thesaurus

Why

To find a synonym or a word to fit a thought

To expand one's vocabulary

To ensure the chosen word is appropriate for the context

What

Groups of words organized according to the ideas they express
and their functions

Features

A comprehensive index is arranged alphabetically but the body of
the book is numbered

Works opposite to a dictionary where you know the word and
want to check the spelling or meaning—in a thesaurus, you
find the word to fit the meaning

Context shapes the selection of words

Headings, subheadings, key or guide words, cross references,
abbreviations

Understanding of word classes and functions is necessary for
economic use of a thesaurus

Trade Publications

Why

To extend the range of clientele

To provide technical information to inside or outside suppliers

To justify the quality of products

What

A range of text forms describing the manufacturing process or the attributes, components, or uses of products or materials

Catalogues, schedules, advertisements, contracts, agreements, specifications, tenders, guarantees, warranties, consumer reports

Features

Technical language

Some for a specific audience, other seeking to expand audience

Trademarks and logos

Diagrams, tables, and schedules

Directions and descriptions

Traditional Tales

Why

To present the case of the oppressed

To show the power of kindness, mercy, and love

To cause reflection on prevailing attitudes

What

Stories with a common structure that have been handed down, generally with an underlying moral or an emphasis on a certain virtue or attribute of human nature

Features

Similar to those listed for folk tales, although culture is not such an important element

Chapter 3

This Text Goes With That One

This chart shows the "umbrella" classification used for this book. Each type can be categorized into subgroups. For example, recipes, directions, instructions, and manuals would be classified as procedural texts.

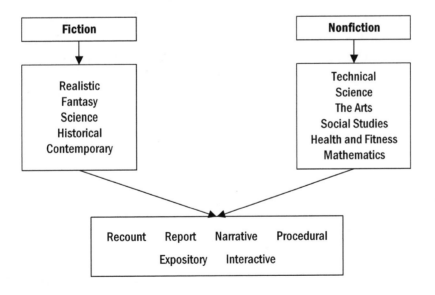

Understandings developed in some of the umbrella writing forms provide a foundation for competence in a range of other forms. For example, reports could be considered an umbrella form. Understanding the key elements of reports will help students learn the features and purposes of other "spokes" of the umbrella.

Understanding the key elements of reports will help students learn the features and purposes of other "spokes" of the umbrella.

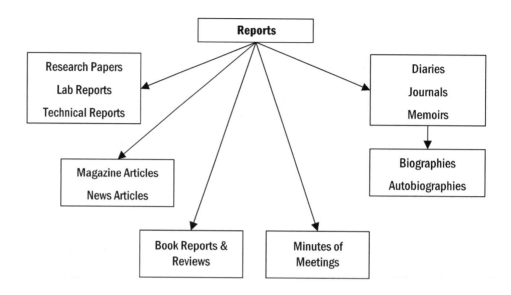

Groups of texts are interdependent, with some overlap in purpose and/or features. Once students are familiar with one text form, it can become the springboard for learning about others or making comparisons.

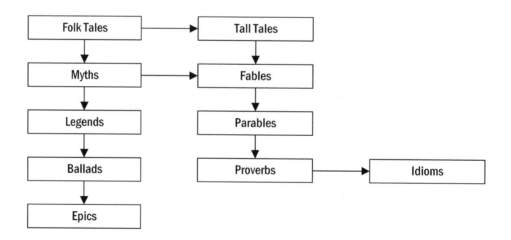

This example shows how groups of text forms can be linked by common elements.

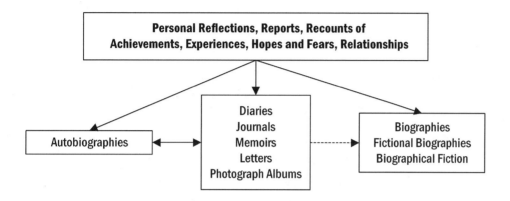

A number of different text forms can also be linked through a common purpose.

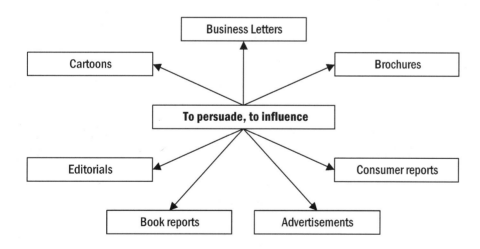

Sometimes more than one form, and a wide range of features, are included within a single publication.

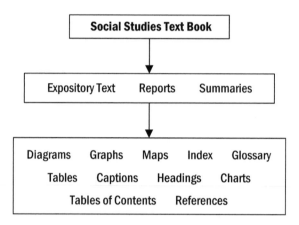

And some texts can be used in conjunction with others, adding more information or detail.

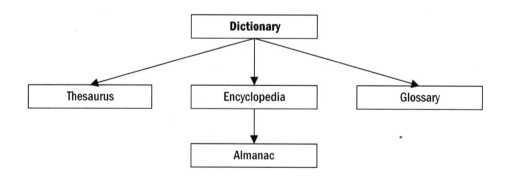

Chapter 4

Voice Within a Text

Every author has a "voice"—a quality difficult to describe but an essential ingredient distinguishing one piece of writing from another. It is the individual way through which an author engages and sustains a reader's commitment to the text. Voice is the author's way of telling a story or presenting information through his or her eyes with the intended audience's ears in mind. It is a combination of the author's attitude toward the topic and theme of the idea, attitude toward those who may read the work, repertoire of techniques to achieve clarity and maintain attention, and craftsmanship in making the pen talk through the printed word.

Just as every writer has an individual voice, so does every piece of writing. No two texts have exactly the same mix of elements. Voice is achieved by the combination of a host of considerations, including choice and combination of words, and the ways these are constructed into larger units to develop and maintain characters, plots, settings, and actions. The plot or structure is carried forward through connected incidents or developments dependent on the way the author creates mood, tension, humor, and suspense.

It would be impossible to list any one author's repertoire of techniques used to create a voice in any one piece. However, the following lists include some of the techniques desirable for students to consider in their writing.

> *Voice is the author's way of telling a story or presenting information through his or her eyes with the intended audience's ears in mind.*

> *It would be impossible to list any one author's repertoire of techniques used to create a voice in any one piece.*

Creating Tension

Change tense

Switch from direct to indirect speech or vice versa

Omit or add adjectival or adverbial phrases to change the pace

Select vocabulary of anxiety or anticipation: in a flash, instantly, immediately, stealthily

Use similes to increase imagery and draw reader into the action

Increase the number of incidents leading to the climax or resolution

Increase the contrast between the attributes of the characters

Repeat words, phrases, incidents

Use imperative verbs in dialogue

Use ellipses

Chapter breaks

Page break

Increase number or size of illustrations

Contrast actions, for example, shout to whisper

Interrupt with a flashback

Increase or change punctuation

Creating Mood

Increase adjectives describing the setting or feelings of characters

Use similes to create images

Use indirect speech

Include character's thoughts

Use present tense

Write in first person

Use impressionistic illustrations

Describe sounds and smells of nature or environment

Use emotive vocabulary

Switch tone suddenly, for example, from humorous to serious

Use extended metaphors

Use personification

Make a sudden change in sentence length or structure

Developing Characters

Make them an essential part of plot and scene development

Show characteristics rather than tell

Show through descriptions, action, and dialogue (see below)

Allows more objective view for reader with third person

Draw reader into more emotional aspects with first person

Include stream of consciousness

Leave something to reader's imagination

Developing Characters Through Dialogue

Include dialect, idioms, and natural speech patterns

Include some interjections or incomplete sentences

Descriptive words or phrases allow reader to "hear" the tone and mood of speech

Use a few words or phrases in several places

Include hand and eye gestures and posture when character is speaking or listening

May use contrasting dialect and vocabulary with one or more other characters to highlight protagonist

Contractions are common

Maintain consistency for credibility

Every piece of dialogue adds to or is true to development of character

Include some emotions in reaction to different situations

Use paragraphing to avoid overuse of descriptors or naming speaker

Include "thought dialogue"

Use dialogue to introduce character

Use dialogue to begin a new incident or chapter

Using Persuasion

Frequently included in résumés, letters (especially letters to the editor or business letters), short stories, biographies, promotional material, brochures, and trade publications to:

    share ideas and stimulate thinking

    explain author's reasons for certain actions or reactions

    prepare reader to accept argument or point of view

May include:

    superlatives

    emotive language

    definitions

    exaggeration

    comparison

    cause and effect

    analogies

    opinion

    personal testimonies

    detailed descriptions

    bias

    statistics

    trick photography

    first or second person rather than third

Assumes reader to be doubtful or antagonistic

Relies on reasoning and logic

Focuses on benefits and strengths

Begins on assumed common or known ground before expressing bias

Anticipates reader's concerns

May include diagrams rather than the truth of photographs

Emotional appeal may be:

> physiological—food, drink, shelter
>
> psychological—need to be accepted and loved, to be
> successful
>
> direct to emotions such as guilt, fear, hate, pride

Often emphasizes long-term benefits (unlikely to be remembered
or checked)

Usually includes positive summary statement

Some Common Story Structures for Young Writers

Cumulative with new idea or information being added at the
beginning, middle, or end of each repeat of basic structure

Interlocking or chain structure—ab, bc, cd—common element is
often a character

Sequential or recount—days of the week, ordinal, increase in
degree or size, natural but obvious order

Alternating—*a* does it, *b* does it, *a* does something else, so does *b*, or
switch between flashback and current, question and answer

Short introduction of problem, predictable number of incidents,
resolution, and quick conclusion, similar to folk tale

One incident, such as fable

Repeated incidents involving one new element (often character,
action, or setting) then twist or element of surprise at end

Repeated incidents requiring the reader to infer ending or fill in
gap before resolution

Chapter 5

Text Features

The reading of many texts is enhanced by an understanding of conventions of layout and text features associated with particular forms of writing. The same conventions and features enable authors to make their ideas and information readily accessible to readers. This chapter provides a quick reference of the purpose and nature of some of these presentation techniques.

Abbreviations

Why

To shorten a word or expression in the following ways:

> contraction, in which one or some letters are omitted but the final letters are included

> when each of several words is represented by its initial letter only

> when the initial letter of two or more words has the phonetic form of a word in its own right (an acronym)

> when usage is frequent and constant, as in references

What

A shortened form of a word or group of words to represent a whole

A substitution for a larger unit of meaning or information

Frequently used for units of measurement of time or weight; for chemical elements; in technical, scientific, scholarly, or musical texts, especially in referencing; in forms of addresses and titles

Features

Appear most frequently in technical texts or in tables, notes, dictionaries, bibliographies, or lists

Usage has increased within technical writing but decreased in formal writing

Some words are almost always abbreviated (e.g., Dr., Mr., Mrs., or measurements of time or weight)

Often spelled out in full at first use and then abbreviated for remainder of text

A period after the shortened form indicates the abbreviation, although this practice is not as common as previously

List of abbreviations used in a text is often included in front or back matter

Italics often used for abbreviated titles

Not used at the beginning of sentences

Plurals often formed by repeating letter (e.g., "pp." for pages)

Acknowledgments

Why

To acknowledge those who have enabled the author to complete the work or to present it in its current format and to cite references to already published material used or reprinted

What

Author's list of thanks is usually contained in the preface or preliminary section of the book unless it is sufficiently extensive to warrant a separate section

Acknowledgment of the use of material from another publication or outside source is a condition of use as well as a courtesy

Acknowledgment of use of other published material is included in main acknowledgment section or the copyright page but also cited on the page containing the relevant material

Features

Acknowledgment of material already published includes author's name, title of work, date and place of publication, publishing house, and an indication that permission has been granted for the work to be included or cited

May include some abbreviations

Set punctuation format according to house style

Often grouped in special section when a number of permissions need to be acknowledged

Appendixes

Why

To explain or elaborate on parts of the text that provide more detail or list references or research for further reading or clarification

What

A supplement to the main body of text, either included in the end matter of a publication or bound separately

A collection of extra or separate material that justifies or provides clarification on parts of a text

Material that would interrupt flow of text but complements or expands specific details within text

Features

Usually placed at the end of the book, though if essential to understanding of a chapter, may be at the end of the chapter

May include tables and charts

May include corrections, new information, examples, supporting or critical information, or cite references

If the main work only presents factual material, the author's opinion may be given in an appendix

A separate appendix may be given to different aspects of the work

Where there is more than one appendix, each is given a number or a letter and begins on a new page

Asterisks

Why

To alert the reader to further information about the marked subject matter

To indicate levels of probability within a table

What

The first in a series of symbols used as reference marks

A star-shaped symbol placed within a text to signal further information, usually as a footnote at the bottom of the page or text

Features

Used to indicate or explain special conditions, doubtful matter, omissions, material from another publication, material explained in other sections of the work

Placed immediately prior to or, more commonly, following the relevant word within running text

Bibliographies

Why

To provide a list of publications on a particular topic

To provide publication details of works cited

To justify or expand on information and ideas presented in main body of text

To provide suggestions for further reading or research

To cite works quoted in text or referenced in preparation of the work

To enable the reader to check on authenticity of quotations or references

What

A list of sources, especially published material, used in the preparation of a work, cited in the work, or relevant to the topic

A list of works by the author of the book

Features

Content for bibliography within a book includes:

> author's last name and initial, given name, or nom de plume
>
> year of publication
>
> title of publication
>
> title of series, if applicable
>
> volume number or number of volumes, if applicable
>
> edition, if applicable
>
> publisher
>
> place of publication
>
> page number or numbers, if applicable

Follow the glossary and precede the index

Often include abbreviations

May be cross-referenced from main text and/or from index

Blurbs

Why

To entice potential buyers or readers

To attract interest

What

A brief promotional description of a work, usually found on the dust jacket or back cover

Features

Usually written by the publisher

May include a hint about the plot or amount and focus of information

Gives some indication of setting, characters, and form of text

May include excerpts of reviews or recommendations

May reference other works by same author

Captions

Why

To explain contents of an object or illustrative material

To summarize visual information

To expand visual information

To give another perspective

To provide a title

To clarify

To identify

What

A title, a headline, or a brief statement (technically called a legend) accompanying an object or illustrative material

The heading or title above an illustration

Features

General framework for captions: Who? What? Where? When? Why? How?

Positioned closer to illustration than to text

May not be a complete sentence, but a caption that is a complete sentence requires a period

May be a subtitle if a caption on television

Often a smaller typeface than main body of text

Chapter Headings

Why

To indicate major divisions within a work

To give a clue about the focus or content of the chapter

To enable readers to scan contents

What

Headings that link or distinguish episodes

Features

Listed in table of contents as well as within book

In texts of considerable length, chapter headings may be grouped into parts or sections

Usually on a new page, and often on a right-hand page

Initial letters capitalized except prepositions, articles, and conjunctions

Usually numbered or titled

If titled may be a cryptic summary of main event in forthcoming chapter

May indicate a new incident or topic or the passage of time

Chapter Summaries

Why

To provide an overview prior to reading or a review at the end of the chapter

To engender further thought or discussion

What

Synopses at the beginning or end of a chapter, usually of a nonfiction work

Sometimes included in the introduction

Features

May be a collection of subheadings or questions or a short summary in continuous text

Common in textbooks as a revision aid

Charts

Why

To record or present information or ideas in a concise form

What

A diagram, list, or table presenting information concisely

Sometimes an on-the-spot recording of ideas or a plan

List showing ratings or sequence

Features

Bullets or numbering

May be jottings or a list

Graphics may be important

Usually headed but may also have an explanatory caption

Usually presented as conclusion, parameters, or expectations

Checklists

Why

To provide an easily accessible reference for recording achievements or progress points

What

Items or names listed for comparison, checking, or assessment

Features

Often set up as a table

May be for cumulative use or as a one-off check

Markings may be a simple check/tick/cross/dash or a quantitative rating

Descriptors of expectation or standards often listed for checking

Entries on checklist may be sequenced in order of challenge or sequence of execution

Codes

Why

To exchange information briefly or secretly

To identify parameters

What

A system of colors, letters, or symbols associated by rules to communicate information

A system of colors, letters, or symbols for identification or selection purposes

A set of written rules determining behavior

Features

If codes are used for brevity, the key may be included below the representation

Often used to represent criteria in a process of selection or evaluation

Computer Menus

Why

To display options within a program

To instruct the program to carry out certain commands

To enable the user to select appropriate commands

What

A pull-down or bar list of icons or symbols of commands representing tasks the computer is able to perform

Features

Menu bar indicates the function of items listed in the pull-down menu

When the menu system is active, a brief description of the function of the command appears on the screen

Usually includes a shortcut code for accessing each command

Indicates which options are available—a shaded command indicates it is unavailable

An ellipsis following a menu command indicates a dialog box

Menu commands can be activated by a mouse or keyboard

Diagrams

Why

To draw attention to specific information

To extend or explain in more detail

To describe the sequence

To identify components

To summarize

To show relativity

To show layout

What

A sketch, plan, or outline demonstrating the form or workings of
   something

A pictorial representation of an object or its parts

Cut-away diagrams, cyclic diagrams, scale diagram, web, tree
   diagram, sequence diagram, Venn diagram

Features

Arrows

Captions

Labels—words out of textual context but pictures provide context

May not be adjacent to relevant section of text

May be inset within or complementary to a larger illustration

Accompanied by a heading or caption

Vocabulary: figure, top/bottom, left/right

Footnotes or Endnotes

Why

To explain a fact or idea

To give the source of a work cited in the body of the text

To direct the reader to further literature on the topic

To cross-reference to other parts of the text

For explanations that would interfere with the main text

What

A note printed at the bottom of a page to which a reference mark or symbol in the body of the text draws attention—they are called notes or endnotes when printed at the end of a chapter or a book

Features

Common in informational or technical texts and sometimes in historical novels explaining details on customs or setting

Numbered consecutively within each chapter

Numbering is usually "superior Arabic"

Reference marks are placed after the word, phrase, or paragraph or number referenced in the footnote or endnote

Endnotes are increasingly preferred to footnotes at bottom of page because of simplicity in typesetting

Forewords

Why

To present an overview of a book or justify why the book is
recommended

What

Short introductory piece to a book written by someone other than
the author—if the introductory piece is written by the author
it is called a preface

Features

Set in same style and size of type as the text

Author's name usually given at end of foreword

May include reaction to the manuscript or support its focus

Often written by eminent person or one knowledgeable in the
topic

Does not contribute to text content

Begins on right-hand page

Glossaries

Why

To provide explanations for words used in a specific context

To explain words unfamiliar because of context or technical specificity

To provide definitions or clarify possible confusions without interrupting the text

What

A list of specialized terms used within a text and an explanation for each relevant to the context of the work

Alphabetical listing of unusual words and definitions at the back of a publication

Features

Usually precedes bibliography and/or index

Arranged alphabetically

New line for each entry

Key word in bold or italicized

Begins on a new page

May include pronunciation guide

Graphs

Why

To present comparative information in a graphical form

To show quantitative relativity of items with a common base

To identify trends or changes

What

A systematic way of presenting statistical information

Proportional representation of data

Types of graphs include pie, line, bar, pictorial, scatter, column, hi-lo

Features

May show more than one set of information

Vocabulary: percentages, anchor points, axes, grid

Both axes should be captioned and, if necessary, extra information included below graph

Headings

Why

To highlight a section or chapter

To summarize the following section

To label a selection

To identify the topic or issue

What

A mini-title for a piece of work, often a piece within a longer work

A word or group of words serving as an indicator or marker

Features

Typography and placement indicates importance

May be a sentence, although this is not usual

Capitalization often follows rules for that of a title

Idioms

Why

To establish familiarity with the reader

To maintain or highlight tone of character, topic, or incident

What

A phrase or grammatical construction that cannot be translated literally into another language

A form of expression unique to a specific group of people or to a language

Ways in which words are commonly combined

Ways in which a specific or identifiable group combine words in a particular context

Features

The meaning may not be predictable from individual words in the expression

Difficult to translate because of unique syntax

The context and the user often define the meaning

Indexes

Why

To enable quick access to specific parts of a text

To enable a reader to cross-check or to gather all information about a topic

To extend the value and use of a publication

What

An expanded table of contents

An alphabetical listing, usually at the end of a book, of persons, works, and topics mentioned in the text, indicating where reference is made

Features

Mainly in nonfiction texts

Entry is the main subdivision, citing the topic, and is followed by a locator, usually the page number, but sometimes chapter and/or section and then the page number

Each entry may have several references and/or a subheading

Main entry is usually in bold type, asterisked, or italicized

Illustrative material may be indicated

Cross-references often included

If material is complex and there are a lot of characters, two indexes will be included

Abbreviations are common

Introductions

Why

To state author's intention

To provide information about what caused work to be written or the purpose and/or focus of the book

To give an idea of the theme and scope of the work and perhaps the setting

What

A short explanatory chapter or paragraph that follows the table of contents

Features

If not written by the author, this section is called a foreword

May include an overview or a succinct summary of the shape of the book

If the author has organized the book into sections, these will be explained

Labels

Why

To identify a place or an object

To claim ownership

To identify a destination

To give brief instructions

To classify an object

What

A brief descriptive term or phrase directing or informing users or viewers of care, use, ownership, or location of an object

A trademark or display of a company or brand name on a product

Features

May be words or phrases rather than complete sentences

Brief descriptors

Usually attached to or placed near subject

Seldom punctuated

Maps (see also Atlases)

Why

To indicate location

To give direction from one place to another

For comparison of position, size, features

What

Pictorial procedural

May indicate street, road, country, land, or oceanic features

May be grouped in an atlas or street directory

Historical map

May be an inset within another text form (e.g., map within a pamphlet or advertisement)

Features

Scale

Longitudinal and latitudinal markings

Compass or part thereof

Specific focus (e.g., location, typography)

Amount of detail varies—reader needs to know how to access more detail

Inferential reading may be required (e.g., significance of route number, or to put part into whole)

Usually includes symbols, some of which may be international

May be linked to an advertisement but usually factual and unbiased

Paragraphs

Why

To divide a longer text into sections for ease of reading

To group ideas or information

To identify a change of speaker

What

A section of continuous text dealing with a single idea or topic and marked by indention or a line space

Features

Can stand alone, but is usually part of a longer work

In expository writing, the first sentence usually identifies the topic or theme of the section, with subsequent sentences expanding or explaining the first. In other writing the last may be the main sentence

Some paragraphs are "framed" with the first and last sentences giving the same main idea but in different words

Rhetorical paragraphs may be one sentence—used to achieve emphasis and variety

Each paragraph has a consistent and specific focus on the subject

When part of a longer work, paragraphs are usually linked by a transition statement or an obvious development

Organization of paragraphs:

> from general to particular
>
> from particular to general
>
> alternating order of general and particular, or pro and con
>
> following order of time
>
> following order of space
>
> building to a climax

Parentheses

Why

To enclose clarifying or explanatory words, phrases, or sentences or those that would interrupt the flow of the text

To enclose numerals marking divisions in a text

What

Brackets that enclose a word or group of words that interrupt a sentence

Features

Parentheses are used to enclose scientific names of plants or animals

Parentheses may fall within a sentence but can sometimes follow a sentence depending on whether it refers to part or the entire sentence

If brackets are not used, paired commas enclose the extra material

Prefaces

Why

To give some explanation about the piece, such as why it was written

To explain how a subsequent edition differs from the original

To introduce the work

To help readers understand the background or structure of the work

What

Introduction to the work written by the author (if it is written by someone else it is a foreword)

Material essential to read before the main body of the work

Features

Each new edition may have a new preface

New preface precedes the original one

In reprints, may include significant corrections that have been made

May include acknowledgments

Placed at beginning of book, after table of contents

Begins on right-hand page

Author's name or initials are placed at the end

Quotation Marks

Why

To identify speech within a text

To denote the beginning and end of a quote from written or oral language

To present dialogue within running text

To draw attention to new or unusual words, words or expressions used in unusual contexts, or to denote technical terms, especially in nontechnical writing

What

Used when referencing titles of chapters, articles, essays, lectures, or songs within a text

Quoted words, phrases, and sentences included in text are enclosed in double quotation marks

Quotations within quotations are enclosed in single quotation marks

The marks denote the beginning and end of speech

Usually immediately preceded or followed by an indication of the speaker

References

Why

To direct attention to a passage elsewhere in the work or to another book or person

What

A coding system indicating the location of other information on the same topic or relevant to the marked item

Features

May appear as footnotes or as bibliographic information

Reference marks often cite other views or expansions of the same view presented elsewhere in the same work

References may be linked to illustrative or graphical material elsewhere in the work

Storyboards

Why

To convert an idea or a written script into a plan for filming

What

Story or outline is divided into individual scenes numbered in sequence

Sequence showing verbal and visual plan or the relationship between the shots and the soundtrack

Features

Layouts include columns or split screen, frames, or script with detailed stage directions

Details include dialogue, camera work, including shot sizes and distance, actors' actions, setting, and props

Story Maps

Why

To plan or review elements and the interdependence of elements of a narrative

What

Usually pictorial webbing identifying the plot, characters, and setting of a story

Features

May be pictorial, words, or phrases

May be based on a set format or a free-flow brainstorming of ideas or facts that are then grouped or sequenced

Usually nouns or references to incidents

Subheadings

Why

To provide quick access to a specific piece of text

To clarify organization of a work

What

The heading or title of a subdivision or subsection of a printed work, usually nonfiction

Short, succinct descriptors of content of a paragraph or small section of text

Features

Usually has a strong link to the first sentence in the following text, which often includes a word from the subheading

Some scientific or technical works require levels of subheadings; these are sometimes numbered

Usually set on a line separate from the text or in the margin (as a shoulder heading or margin entry)

Sometimes used as running heads

Subtitles

Why

To provide further explanation of the content, form, or focus of the work

What

Supplementary part of main title

Features

May only be used in some contexts or positions, e.g., on title page but not on cover or in running heads

May explain form or focus of work

Symbols

Why

To represent information briefly

What

A sign or character representing a word or words

An object, person, or an idea used to suggest or represent something else

Features

May bear little or no resemblance to the word or words it represents

Graphics rather than orthographics are usually important

Tables

Why

To present data for comparison in a succinct form

What

A framework for collecting, recording, and comparing data

An economical method of providing readers of a nonfiction book with detailed, often numerical, information

Features

Often includes numerical information

Supported by a heading and/or caption

Often cited as a figure (Figure; fig.)

Vocabulary: cells, rows

Reader often left to draw own conclusions or to test conclusions of others

May provide more detail to sections of text

Best tables are simple—too much information confuses the purpose

When more than one table is included in a work, each is numbered

Title should clearly indicate purpose of table

Caption should include source of information

Tables of Contents

Why

To show how a book is organized

To provide an overview

To allow quick access to specific parts

To help the reader decide where to begin reading

To give an indication of the form and style of writing

To list contributors

To give an indication of the length of each chapter or section

What

A sequential list of items or divisions within the work

Gives title and beginning page number of each section of a book

Features

May include subsections, particularly in technical books

When subheadings are used, they are indented

Page numbers usually flush on right-hand side of page

If a number of contributors, authors' names will be included

Timetables

Why

To provide information about the time of events

To maintain a sequence, order, or schedule

What

A list or table of events arranged in a chronological sequence

Features

Usually presented as a table or vertical list

Abbreviations, especially A.M. and P.M.

May be based on 24-hour clock

Span of time often indicated with en dash (–) or hyphen

Asterisks

May represent daily, weekly, monthly, or yearly schedules

Titles

Why

To attract attention

To entice the reader into the work

To identify the focus and/or the form of the content

To establish the uniqueness of a work

What

The name of a work

Features

Two main systems—maximal, where the first letter of the first and all other words except articles are capitalized, and minimal, where only the first letter of the first word and the first letter of words normally capitalized are in upper case

A title proper includes any subtitle

Title of a full-length work mentioned in a text is in italics

Title within a text may be abbreviated when full title is included in footnote or bibliography

A period is not used to indicate the end of a title

Title Pages

Why

To provide further general information about the work

To entice readers to select the book

What

Presents the full title (including subtitle, if any), author's name, and usually publisher's name and location—children's books also list the illustrator and may have an illustration

Features

May include an illustration, especially in a children's book

Bibliography

Baldick, Chris. 1990. *The Concise Oxford Dictionary of Literary Terms*. London, England: Oxford University Press.

Cox, Alan, Linda Burgess, and Sandra Mohekey. 1996. *Writing and Presenting*. Auckland, New Zealand: Addison Wesley Longman New Zealand Limited.

Cuddon, A. J. 1992. *The Penguin Dictionary of Literary Terms and Literary Theory*, 3/e. London, England: Penguin Books.

Frye, Northrop, Sheridan Baker, George Perkins, and Barbara M. Perkins. 1997. *The Harper Handbook to Literature*, 2/e. White Plains, NY: Longman.

Kenny, Ann. 1996. *Night Walk*. Katonah, NY: Richard C. Owen Publishers, Inc.

May, Jill P. 1995. *Children's Literature & Critical Theory*. New York, NY: Oxford University Press.

Mooney, Margaret E. In press. *Intentional Teaching: Guided Reading Beyond Grade 3*. Katonah, NY: Richard C. Owen Publishers, Inc.

Rountree, Kathryn. 1998. *Writing for Success*. Auckland, New Zealand: Longman.

Sorenson, Sharon. 1997. *Webster's New World Student Writing Handbook*, 3/e. New York, NY: Macmillan.

Tomlison, Carl M., and Carol Lynch-Brown. 1996. *Essentials of Children's Literature,* 2/e. Boston, MA: Allyn and Bacon.

The University of Chicago Press. 1982. *The Chicago Manual of Style*, 13/e. Chicago, IL: The University of Chicago Press.

Williamson, Hugh. 1983. *Methods of Book Design,* 3/e. New Haven, CT: Yale University Press.

Index

*Rach —
I didn't even look at it. I'll borrow it later... maybe last block after your demo I'll take notes.*
Thanks!